TRADITIONAL COUNTRY LIFE RECIPE SERIES

PUMPKIN

COMPANION

TRADITIONAL COUNTRY LIFE RECIPE SERIES

PUMPKIN
COMPANION

Recipes by
Elizabeth Brabb with
special thanks to Helen Krupski, Krupski Farms,
for her contributions to this project.

History by
Bruce T. Paddock

Interior Illustrations   *Cover Illustration*
Alison Gail   Lisa Adams

The Brick Tower Press ®
1230 Park Avenue, New York, NY 10128
Copyright © 1996
Recipes by Elizabeth Brabb; History by Bruce T. Paddock

Brabb, Elizabeth
Paddock, Bruce
The Traditional Country Life Recipe Series:
Includes Index
ISBN 1-883283-08-6 softcover

Library of Congress Catalog Card
Number: 95-80493
First Edition, December 1996

TABLE OF CONTENTS

According to Captain John Smith, the Indians of Virginia "plant amongst the corn pumpions, and a fruit like unto our muskmelon, but less and worse, which they call macocks."

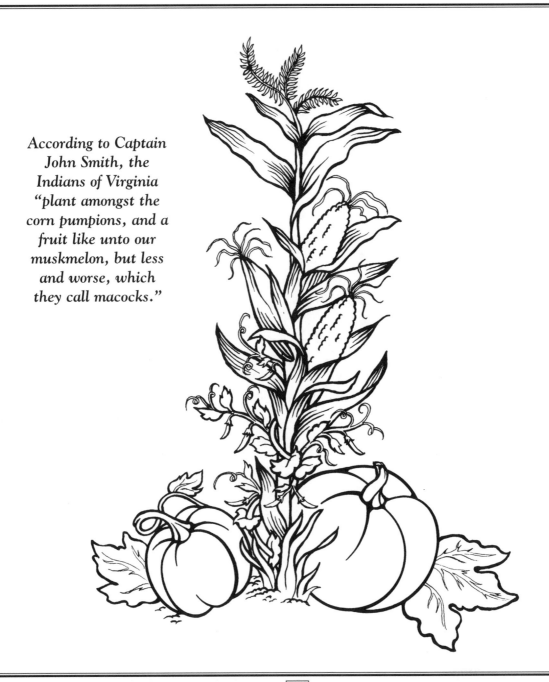

PUMPKINS, PUMPKINS

The history of the pumpkin is harder to trace than you might think. The first problem is that it's surprisingly hard to define exactly what a pumpkin is. Pumpkins belong to the genus *Cucurbita*. Within this genus are four species: *C. maxima*, *C. moshcata*, *C. mixta*, and *C. pepo*. Now here's the tricky part. A pumpkin can belong to any one of those four species. So can just about any kind of winter squash.

A pumpkin is basically just any squash that is round and orange and has orange flesh. *The New York Botanical Garden Illustrated Encyclopedia of Horticulture* has a definition of a pumpkin that is wonderfully teleological and very nearly tautological. According to this book, a pumpkin is a plant that has "large, usually more or less spherical fruits, orange when ripe, that when fully mature are used for making pies and jack-o'-lanterns and as stock feed." So if you make a jack o' lantern out of it, it is, by definition, a pumpkin.

Two jack-o-'lanterns

Next, the researcher faces this the problem of translation. If one of Pliny's* writings makes reference to a "pumpkin," was it really a pumpkin, or just a poor choice of

---

* *Pliny the Elder, A.D. c.23-A.D.79, Roman naturalist. Author of an encyclopedia of science called "Historic naturalis."*

words by the translator? In one document—a translation of a 17th-century Dutch explorer's writing—one vegetable is referred to as a "pumpkin" in one sentence and a "gourd" in the very next sentence. Granted, a pumpkin is a gourd (*Cucurbita* is part of the gourd family, *Cucurbitaceae*). But really, this whole situation could be a lot clearer.

Most people think that pumpkins are uniquely American. However, there is strong evidence that *C. maxima* was growing wild in Africa long before Europeans or Americans got there. Of course, it's very hard to say whether any of those indigenous African *C. maxima* grew big and round and orange. Either way, one school of thought has it that *Cucurbita* in general developed in Africa and then moved to the New World. If so, this happened quite some time ago; gourd seeds have been found in Mexican archaeological sites that date back to 7000 B.C.

Of course, the big question is: How might the gourds have gotten from Africa to the Americas? Well, they could have floated. It's a rare plant that can fall into the ocean, wash up on a shore thousands of miles away, and then germinate. But it does happen, and, over a span of tens of thousands of years, not infrequently. The problem is gourds usually do not grow anywhere near the shoreline. In addition, there are plenty of small crustaceans at the shore that like to drill inside debris and eat the contents. Not a problem for a coconut, which is too hard to get into, or a tuber like the potato, with its eyes on the outside. But a fruit with a penetrable rind and seeds on the inside would be destroyed by these creatures as soon as it is washed up.

There might be an easier solution. The yam also made its way from Africa to the Americas, and the yam doesn't float. Therefore, it was probably carried across the ocean by humans. The eastern tip of South America is only about 1,800 miles from the western tip of Africa, and Thor Heyerdahl's Ra-2 expedition proved that ancient Egyptians could have sailed to the West Indies. If they did, did they have

Maybe gourds floated their way from Africa to the Americas...

gourds to bring with them? Gourd seeds have been found in 12th-Dynasty Egyptian tombs—but the 12th Dynasty started around 1900 B.C., long after gourds had arrived in the Americas. Earlier dynasties may have had them, too, but we don't know.

We do know that ancient Americans sailed as far west as Polynesia. It is possible that C. *maximus* made its way from Africa, across the Indian Ocean and part of the Pacific, to meet up with Americans visiting the islands there. But, for now at least, the answer to the question "Did people bring *Cucurbita* to the New World?" must remain, "Possibly."

And there is even another possibility. Whether the trip between the Americas and Africa was made in a boat or floating on ocean currents, it might have occurred in the opposite direction. The plants might have originated in the Americas, and then, one way or another, made their way to Africa.

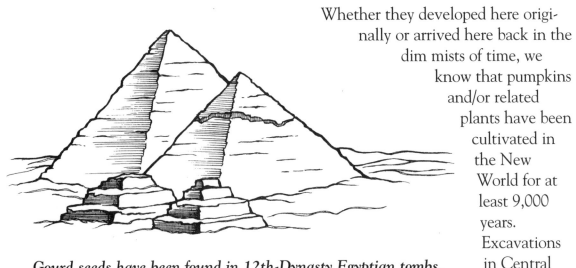

Whether they developed here originally or arrived here back in the dim mists of time, we know that pumpkins and/or related plants have been cultivated in the New World for at least 9,000 years. Excavations in Central and South America have turned up so much of the fibrous squash material that archaeologists are fairly sure it formed a large portion of the native diet. In fact, scientists claim they can determine from the remains they've found that the Native Americans ate the squashes when they were immature, and ate them whole as well.

Gourd seeds have been found in 12th-Dynasty Egyptian tombs.

Of course, food wasn't the only thing that pumpkins and other squash were used for. Pre-Columbian Native Americans from Peru to Mexico to Colorado used them as bottles, bowls, and dishes. The stems were used as bottle stoppers. Large ones were dried, cleaned out, and used as water pails, or as storage bins for grains and seeds.

Mind you, Native Americans weren't the only ones who were aware of the utilitarian delights of these plants. Ancient Greeks and Romans also used them as bottles, carriers, and storage containers. Translators of ancient documents use the terms "pumpkin," "melon," marrow," and "gourd," but what plants were actually used 2–3,000 years ago in this part of the world? We will probably never know.

Pliny the Elder writes of eating one of these vegetables by scraping away the rind to get at the flesh. He also, apparently, ate the stem. Clearly, this wasn't a pumpkin. On the other hand, he also wrote of a "giant cucumber," which is usually taken to mean a pumpkin. On the other hand, it was during Pliny's lifetime (the first half of the first century A.D.) that the "melopepo" was developed—somewhat serendipitously, apparently. This plant had fruit that was described as being round and golden and as trailing along the ground (rather than hanging down like cucumbers). This could have been a form of pumpkin…or it could simply have been a melon.

Pre-Columbian Native Americans from Peru to Mexico to Colorado used pumpkins and squash for bottles, bowls, and dishes.

Whatever pumpkins, squash, or gourds the Ancient Greeks and Romans had, they were undoubtedly brought from the interior of Africa. But as the great Mediterranean empires collapsed, trade with the interior of the continent dried up. As time went on, Europeans forgot about gourds, squashes, and—if they ever knew them—pumpkins.

When European culture resurfaced several hundred years later, they might have rediscovered the bounty that inland Africa had to offer. However, their eyes were drawn, not toward Africa, but toward Asia and the Middle East. These lands were controlled by the Ottoman Turks, who were, of course, Muslims, and the sworn enemies of Christian Europeans. In addition, by the end of the 1500s the Ottomans had the largest empire on the planet, so they could pretty much make life difficult for whomever they felt like.

The two worst blows came in 1453, when the Ottomans captured Constantinople—thus bringing about the end of the Holy Roman Empire—and in 1456, when they captured Athens. Spiritual Europeans were upset because they didn't feel that the Holy Land should be governed by non-Christians. Pragmatic Europeans were upset because the capture of Athens blocked access to the Middle East—and to the lands beyond: the Indies, with all their spices.

It may seem odd to us today to get all excited about a little pepper and some cardamom, but look at some figures. A trader could buy 3,000 tons of spices in the Indies for £91,041, then sell them back in Europe for £789,168. Even after you subtract the cost of a ship, supplies, and salaries for the crew, that's quite a hefty profit. No wonder Columbus wanted to find a better way to the Indies. (Actually, these figures are from 1621; it was harder to get spices before, say, 1490, so the profit margin would probably have been even higher.)

Maybe humans brought gourds with them on ancient sailing ships like the one created for Thor Heyerdahl's Ra-2 expedition.

Despite what your Social Studies teacher taught you, most people in 1492 knew that the world was round. Their disagreement with Columbus was over the size of it. And, of course, Columbus was wrong. He thought that the Indies were just on the other side of the Atlantic Ocean, about 3–4,000 miles from Europe. Everyone else thought, rightly, that they were much farther away. And if the Americas hadn't existed, the Nina, the Pinta, and the Santa Maria would have kept sailing west into oblivion, their crews having died long before they could have reached land.

But the Americas did exist, and Columbus bumped smack into them. It wasn't until his second voyage to the Caribbean that he realized he wasn't in the Indies that everyone knew and loved; and it seems unlikely he ever figured out that he hadn't reached Asia. But he hadn't. He had found a new world, full of new peoples and new foods: maize, beans, tomatoes, peppers (different types from those already known), turkeys, peanuts, potatoes, guavas, bananas, avocados, sweet potatoes…and pumpkins.

Economics dictated Columbus's discovery of the New World, and with it, "pumpkins."

Just about everywhere in Central and North America, pumpkins were a staple of the Native American diet. The three mainstays (or four, depending upon what part of the continent you were in and which European was doing the recording) of any Native American village were corn, beans, and pumpkins (and perhaps squash).

Here is Cabeza de Vaca, describing what he found as he traveled through Mexico in the early 1530s:

"…fine dwellings of civilization, whose inhabitants lived on beans and pumpkins."

Hernando DeSoto, traveling through Florida in 1539, found that

"…beans and pumpkins were in great plenty; both were larger and better than those of Spain; the pumpkins when roasted had nearly the taste of chestnuts."

According to John Smith, the Indians of Virginia

"…plant amongst the corn pumpions, and a fruit like unto our muskmelon, but less and worse, which they call macocks."

Nearly 300 years later, New Englander W. Strachey explained what macocks were: "Macocks is of the form of our pumpions—I must confess nothing so good—of a more waterish taste."

A Dutch settler in the northeast wrote in about 1650:

Seeds

"The natives have another species of this vegetable peculiar to themselves, called by our people quasiens, a name derived from the aborigines.…They do not wait for it to ripen before making use of the fruit, but only until it has attained a certain size. They gather the quasiens, and immediately place them on the fire without any further trouble.…"

The vegetable in question here was the squash—*quasiens* being the Dutch name. The English name is a truncation of the Algonquian word *askutasquash*, meaning "eaten raw." The word pumpkin, by the way, probably comes from the French word *pompon*, which means "melon."

Ulysses P. Hedrick, in his *A History of Horticulture in America*, points out that Native American agriculture lagged behind that of Europeans for two reasons. They had no beasts of burden to haul soil, fertilizer, or produce (yes, South America had the llama; but only in the Andes, where the terrain isn't suited for large-scale agriculture); and, especially in North America, there was such an overabundance of game that they didn't have to rely on produce. Still, they did rely on corn, beans, squash, and pumpkins (the squash flower was even a symbol of fertility to the Hopi), and the agricultural techniques they used were oftentimes quite clever.

Just about everywhere on the continent, all three (or four) of the staples were planted in the same fields. Beans were planted in the same hills as corn, and the bean plants used the corn stalks for support. Squash and pumpkins, meanwhile, were planted between the hills. The Hurons had even found a way to extend the growing season by forcing pumpkin seeds. They would gather rotted wood from decaying tree stumps, powder it, and place it in a box made of tree bark. They would plant the seeds in the wood powder, then hang the box over a low, smoky fire. The smoke would gradually warm the wood powder, and the seeds would sprout in just a few days.

As soon as the arriving Europeans were introduced to pumpkins, they immediately started shipping them, and their seeds, back to Europe. From there, they went just about everywhere. In China, it was the custom to make an offering of foodstuffs to one's ancestors at the beginning of each month (or, more precisely, at each new moon). We have a list of what comprised each sacrifice in the emperor's household for each month of the year 1590. The offerings were supposed to represent ordinary family life, so it's a good bet that they can tell us what was actually eaten in the imperial household at various times of the year. The offering for the 5th month consisted of shad, wheat noodles, barley grains, wheat grains, pullets, peaches and plums, haw apples, eggplant, wild lettuce, gourds…and pumpkins.

However, as DeSoto pointed out above, pumpkins never taste quite as good when they're planted outside their native soil. And here in America, colonists took to them with the same enthusiasm that the natives had. And no one took to them with more enthusiasm than the colonists of New England. They made sauces from pumpkins, they stewed it with cider to make pumpkin butter, they dried it for winter, they made several kinds of pie from it, and they even made bread from it (mixed half-and-half with cornmeal). During the Revolution, when sugar and molasses were scarce, colonists found ways to make sugar and sweet syrup from pumpkins.

Incidentally, colonial pumpkin pie was not what you might ordinarily think of as a pie. To make it, one would cut a hole in the top of the pumpkin; scoop out the seeds and such inside; stuff it with apples, spices, sugar, and milk; then stick it in the fire to bake. Flour was often scarce in the New England colonies, and this technique was probably developed as a way to save it. Those who had enough flour may very well have made ordinary pies.

So dependent on pumpkins were these New England colonists that Edward Johnson, writing in 1654, called it "a fruit which the Lord fed his people with till corn and cattle increased." One writer of the late colonial period, relating a story that had occurred some years back, referred to "the times when old Pompion was a saint." And a verse from the period underscores, in no uncertain terms, how important pumpkins were to the settlers.

For pottage and puddings and custard and pies,
Our Pumpkins and parsnips are common supplies;
We have pumpkin at morning and pumpkin at noon;
If it were not for pumpkin we should be undone.

Every state fair in the country has a contest for the largest this or the biggest that. Pumpkins are usually the biggest of the big.

Interestingly, the pumpkin actually enters into New England colonial politics in at least two instances. The earliest colonists were, of course, Puritans and other separatists, seeking to set up communities based on their own beliefs and laws, rather than on those of the Church of England, which dominated back home. However, they were soon joined in the New World by loyal Anglican colonists, and the disagreements between the two groups continued.

When a group of Puritans formed the New Haven colony in 1638, one of their original laws was that every male had to have his hair cut short. You see, Levitical law, which the Anglicans apparently followed, forbade the cutting of hair or the rounding of the head. So the Puritan men cut their hair—using the time-honored method of placing a cap on the head and cutting off everything that stuck out beyond it. If a cap were not available, so the story goes, a pumpkin was used instead. So the Anglicans often referred to the Puritans derisively as "pumpkin-heads." In addition, the Puritans celebrated Thanksgiving, while the Anglicans did not. They even went so far as to call the holiday, again derisively, "St. Pumpkin's Day."

So time passed, the colonies prospered, Americans' diets were expanded, and pumpkins fell from their position of prominence. Nowadays, for those not fortunate enough to own this book, pumpkins are used pretty much only for pie filling and jack o'lanterns. (Interesting fact that fits nowhere else: Victorians made jack o'lanterns by cutting out the back of the pumpkin, not the top. In fact, they cut out a sort of a keyhole shape—wide on the bottom with its narrow part sticking up—

that could just accommodate a candle and its holder. Supposedly this technique improves the air flow through the jack o'lantern, letting the candle flame burn stronger with less possibility of being blown out. The fact that they would actually scrape out all of the pumpkin's insides through this small opening tells you that life was far more slowly paced back then—or that most people had (or were) servants.) Anyway, nowadays pumpkins are used pretty much only for pie filling and jack o'lanterns. Is this, then, the end of the story?

Not at all. The story of the pumpkin continues on two fronts. The first involves the seeds. Many people like to eat pumpkin seeds. But the seeds are surrounded by an inedible hull. It would be much easier to eat them—and much cheaper to sell them—if they didn't have the hull around them. An Austrian researcher discovered the gene coding for hull-less seeds back in 1933, and Eastern Europeans have been growing hull-less-seeded squashes ever since (squash seed oil and pumpkin seed oil are much more important commodities there than they are here). But these genetically-altered plants produce very few seeds, and the ones they do produce are quite small.

Brent Loy, a plant breeder at the University of New Hampshire in Durham, spent 11 years working on this problem. The standard technique was to breed larger pumpkins—larger pumpkins, more seeds, right? Loy, however, ended up going the other way. In 1993, he succeeded in creating a small pumpkin (5 inches in diameter, 1 1/2 pounds) that produces 3–400 hull-less seeds. You can dry them, salt them, or pop them like popcorn in the microwave.

The other area in which pumpkin development continues is size. Every state fair in the country has a contest for the largest this or the biggest that. Pumpkins, of course, are usually the biggest of the big. (Another interesting fact that sort of fits here: When Captain Cook first landed on the Hawaiian Islands, he found a type of pumpkin that the natives called *ipu nui*, which held 10–12 gallons. Sadly, it's now extinct.)

In 1993 (apparently a banner year for pumpkins), a factory worker from Winthrop, New York, named Donald Black grew an 884-pound pumpkin. He drove 22 hours to Nova Scotia in order to enter it in a contest. Not surprisingly, it won. Black received $4000, plus $1250 for every weekend it was displayed (in California, for some reason), plus a free trip to California in order to visit his pumpkin.

What do you need to do if you want to grow a superpumpkin? Well, let's start with the basics. Pick a spot that gets full sunlight throughout the day. You'll want to plant your pumpkins 6 to 10 feet apart, so you'll need a lot of space. (There are varieties of pumpkins on the market that grow on bushes, not vines, and so require much less groundspace in the garden. But these kinds don't get very big—for obvious reasons.) For each plant, dig a hole 18 inches deep and 24 inches across. Fill the hole with loose soil that has been heavily mixed with compost or seasoned manure. Fill until it mounds a couple of inches above the surface of the garden. Plant several seeds in each mound, about 3/4 of an inch deep.

Pumpkins, gourds, and the smell of fresh flowers con-
tribute to an autumn harvest at Lawrence Farms,
Newburgh, New York.

If you want, you can soak the seeds overnight before planting them, in order to has-
ten germination. Pumpkins grow best in temperatures between 64° F. and 86° F., and
they get damaged if the temperature falls below 50° F., so depending on the climate
where you are, you may want to start them indoors. If you do, plant several seeds in
each of a number of small, individual pots—you don't want to disturb the roots
when you transplant them.

You should soon have several sprouts per hill (or pot). Let them grow for about a week, then pluck all but the largest, strongest one in each hill (or pot). In order to get the largest fruits possible, you want to make sure that plants never need for water. They are, fortunately, deep-rooted plants, but it can't hurt to keep an eye on the moisture content of the soil. Also, fertilize them about once a month, or maybe even a little more frequently.

The plants will produce flowers in two shifts. The first set will be male, the second will probably be mixed male and female (the female flowers are the ones with the small fruits below them). In order for pumpkins to grow, the pollen has to get from the male flowers to the female flowers. You can rely on bees for this, or you can take matters into your own hands—literally. Wait until the female flowers open (they'll only be open for one day), then gently pluck the male flowers and dab them inside the females.

Pests may be a problem, especially when the plants are small. One way to protect them involves a cardboard box about 18 inches square and 12 inches high. Cut out the bottom of the box, replace it with cheesecloth, and set it over the plants. You can accomplish the same thing by stretching the cheesecloth over stakes set around the plant. Either way, be sure to remove them as soon as the plants outgrow them.

Again, to insure the largest pumpkins possible, pluck all but one, or perhaps two, on each vine. You might want to consider cutting off the vine 4–5 feet beyond the fruit. Be sure to trim any foliage that shades the fruit. Keep fertilizing, watch the water, and see how big they'll grow!

If you're growing for size, there are several varieties of pumpkin to try. Big Max and King of the Mammoths are popular, while the current record holder is an Atlantic Giant. It should be pointed out, though, that the largest pumpkins are seldom the

The pumpkin harvest at Krupski Farms,
Peconic, New York, is an annual tradition.

best tasting pumpkins. Their flesh is too coarse, and not very flavorful. (These varieties are, however, frequently grown for the canning market. Canned "pumpkin" often also consists of a fair amount of non-pumpkin squash. Two more reasons not to buy canned pumpkin filling.) If you want to throw in a couple for the kids to make jack o'lanterns with, try Half Moon, Connecticut Field, Ghost Rider, Tallman, or, not surprisingly, Jack O'Lantern.

If however, you want to try out the recipes in this book (and believe me, you do), try the Small Sugar, Spirit, or Autumn Gold varieties. They produce medium-sized fruits with great flavor. The Jack O'Lantern varieties listed above don't taste too bad, either. Or you might want to try some of the smaller varieties, like Sweetie Pie, Baby Pam, or Little Lantern. They're usually grown for ornamental purposes, but they can be used for cooking, too—especially if you're short of growing space.

There's a new variety on the market that you might want to try, too. It's called Triple Treat, and it's supposed to have tasty flesh and make a good jack o'lantern…and it has hull-less seeds that are ready for roasting right out of the pumpkin. Who could ask for more?

And now, gentle reader, our time together is through. I hope I've managed to pique your interest and whet your appetite. Here I'll turn you over to Ms. Brabb who will deliver the goods. Enjoy!

Bruce T. Paddock
New York, 1996.

SOME COOKING TIPS

For baking:

Preheat the oven to 350° F

(1) Cut the squash in half.
(2) Pour a small amount of water into a baking pan.
(3) Place the squash, cut side down, in the baking pan.
(4) Bake until fork tender.
(5) Scoop out the squash with a spoon; discard the skin.

For the Microwave:

(1) Poke holes in the squash with a fork.
(2) Place on a microwavable dish.
(3) Microwave on high for 10 minutes.
(4) Turn the squash and continue cooking in the microwave for another five minutes.
(5) Repeat until the squash is fork tender.
(6) Scoop out the squash with a spoon; discard the skin.

For boiling:

(1) Peel the squash with a vegetable peeler.
(2) Cut the squash into cubes.
(3) Bring a large pot of lightly salted water to a boil.
(4) Carefully place the squash into the pot of boiling water.
(5) Cover and boil until the squash is fork tender.
(6) Drain the squash in a colander.
(7) Mash the squash with a potato masher.

PECAN PUMPKIN MUFFINS
STUFFED WITH CHEESE

Preheat the oven to 400° F.

(1) Grease muffin pans.
(2) In a large bowl, mix flour, sugar, pecans, pumpkin pie spice, baking powder, and salt.
(3) In a small bowl, combine the eggs, pumpkin, butter, and sour cream.
(4) Add the pumpkin mixture to the flour mixture and stir just until blended.
(5) Fill the greased muffin pans until they are one-third full.
(6) Place a cube of cream cheese in the center of each.
(7) Add enough batter to fill pans two-thirds full.
(8) Combine cinnamon and sugar.
(9) Sprinkle tops with cinnamon sugar mixture.
(10) Bake for 20 to 25 minutes or until a cake tester comes out clean when inserted in the center of a muffin.

INGREDIENTS

2 cups of flour
1/2 cup of sugar
1/2 cup of chopped pecans
1 tablespoon of baking powder
1 1/2 teaspoon of pumpkin pie spice
1/2 teaspoon of salt
2 eggs, slightly beaten
3/4 cup of cooked pumpkin purée
1/2 cup butter, melted
1/4 cup of sour cream
3 ounces of cream cheese, cut in cubes
cinnamon
sugar

MAKES 12 MUFFINS

PUMPKIN BRAN MUFFINS

Preheat the oven to 425° F.

(1) Grease muffin pans.
(2) In a large bowl, combine oat bran cereal, brown sugar, baking powder, salt, and rosemary.
(3) In a small bowl, mix the pumpkin purée, milk, eggs, and oil.
(4) Add the pumpkin mixture to the flour mixture and stir just until blended.
(5) Fill the greased muffin pans until they are full.
(6) Bake for 20 to 25 minutes or until a cake tester comes out clean when inserted in the center of a muffin.

INGREDIENTS

2 cups of oat bran cereal
1/4 cup of brown sugar
2 teaspoons of baking powder
1/2 teaspoon of salt
1/2 teaspoon of rosemary
1 cup of pumpkin purée
1 cup of milk
2 eggs, lightly beaten
2 tablespoons of oil

MAKES 8 MUFFINS

PUMPKIN PANCAKES

(1) Mix the all-purpose flour, whole wheat flour, baking powder, salt, sugar, and cinnamon in a large bowl.

(2) Beat together the egg, butter, and pumpkin purée.

(3) Add the pumpkin mixture, and buttermilk, to the flour mixture to make a batter a little thicker than the buttermilk. Add more buttermilk if necessary.

(4) Heat a large skillet or griddle and brush with oil.

(5) When the surface is very hot, pour a small amount of the batter onto the griddle for each pancake and cook until small bubbles appear and begin to break

(6) Flip each pancake and cook on other side until golden.

(7) Serve immediately with butter and maple syrup.

INGREDIENTS

1 cup of all-purpose flour
1/2 cup of whole wheat flour
1 teaspoon of baking powder
1/2 teaspoon of salt
1 tablespoon of sugar
1/2 teaspoon of cinnamon
1 extra large egg
2 tablespoons of butter, melted
1 cup of cooked pumpkin puree
1 cup of buttermilk
oil
sugar
butter
maple syrup, warmed

SERVES 4

BUTTERCUP-APPLESAUCE
PANCAKES

(1) Mix together the flour salt, baking powder, cinnamon, nutmeg, and sugar.

(2) Lightly beat the eggs.

(3) Combine the eggs, squash, applesauce, milk, butter, and vanilla extract. Add more milk if the batter is too thick.

(4) Heat a large skillet or griddle and brush with oil.

(5) When the surface is very hot, pour a small amount of the batter onto the griddle for each pancake and cook until small bubbles appear and begin go break.

(6) Flip each pancake and cook on the other side until golden.

(7) Serve immediately with butter and maple syrup.

◈ INGREDIENTS

2 1/2 cups of all-purpose flour
1/2 teaspoon of salt
2 teaspoons of baking powder
1 teaspoon of cinnamon
1/2 teaspoon of nutmeg
1/2 cup of sugar
4 eggs
1 cup of buttercup squash purée
2 cups of applesauce
1/4 cup of milk
2 tablespoons of butter, melted
1 1/2 teaspoons of vanilla
 extract
butter
maple syrup, warmed

SERVES 4

BUTTERNUT-WALNUT WAFFLES

(1) In a small bowl, sift together the flour, baking powder, salt, and sugar.
(2) In a large bowl, lightly beat the egg yolks.
(3) To the egg yolks, add the butternut squash, walnuts, Half and Half, and butter; combine until just blended.
(4) Beat the egg whites until soft peaks form.
(5) Gently fold the egg whites into the batter.
(6) Heat a waffle iron.
(7) Lightly brush the waffle iron with oil.
(8) Pour a quarter cup of batter into the center of the waffle iron; cover.
(9) Cook until the waffle iron stops steaming.
(10) Serve with butter and maple syrup.

INGREDIENTS

1 1/2 cups of flour
3 teaspoons of baking powder
1/2 teaspoon of salt
2 teaspoons of sugar
3 eggs, separated
1/2 cup of cooked butternut squash purée
1/2 cup of finely chopped walnuts
1 1/2 cups of Half and Half
3 tablespoons of butter, melted butter
maple syrup, warmed

SERVES 4

STUFFED CHEESE OMELET

(1) Combine the eggs and water and beat until blended.

(2) Peel and thinly slice the apple. Cut each slice in half.

(3) Melt 1 tablespoon of butter in a small skillet.

(4) Add the apple slices and sauté until the apple is tender.

(5) Remove from the heat and add the squash and nutmeg; combine.

(6) Melt the remaining tablespoon of butter in a hot 10-inch skillet.

(7) Add the eggs and reduce heat to medium.

(8) Spread the apple-squash mixture over half of the omelet.

(9) Top half of omelet with the cheese.

(10) Cover and cook omelet for approximately 6 minutes.

(11) When the omelet is cooked remove from the heat and fold in half onto a warmed serving platter.

INGREDIENTS

4 eggs
4 tablespoons of water
1 small McIntosh apple
2 tablespoons of butter
1/2 cup of cooked butternut squash purée
1/8 teaspoon of nutmeg
3/4 cup of grated medium sharp Cheddar cheese

SERVES 2

PUMPKIN FRENCH TOAST

(1) Combine pumpkin purée, butter, eggs, brown sugar, nutmeg, cinnamon, and milk.
(2) Slice bread into 1/2-inch slices.
(3) Pour 1/3 of the liquid into two 12x9x2-inch baking dishes.
(4) Place bread slices into the baking dishes.
(5) Pour the remaining liquid over the bread.
(6) Cover and refrigerate overnight.

Preheat the oven 350° F.

(7) Remove baking dishes from the refrigerator, uncover, and bring to room temperature if glass.
(8) Bake for 50-60 minutes.
(9) Meanwhile whip heavy cream until slightly thickened.
(10) Add vanilla extract and sugar and beat until soft peaks form.
(11) Remove French toast from oven and top each serving with whipped cream and raspberry jam.

INGREDIENTS

1 cup of cooked pumpkin purée
9 tablespoons of butter, melted
8 eggs, lightly beaten
1/2 cup of brown sugar, firmly packed
1/4 teaspoon of nutmeg
1/4 teaspoon of cinnamon
3 cups of milk
2 loaves of Italian bread
2 cups of heavy whipping cream
2 teaspoons of vanilla extract
1 tablespoon of sugar
raspberry jam

SERVES 10

PUMPKIN BREAD

Preheat the oven to 350° F.

(1) In a large bowl, combine, sugar, pumpkin purée, oil, and eggs.
(2) Sift together flour, baking powder, baking soda, salt, cloves, nutmeg, cinnamon, and allspice.
(3) Add the flour mixture to the pumpkin mixture and stir until combined.
(4) Add the water, raisins, and nuts; and stir until blended.
(5) Pour the batter into two greased loaf pans.
(6) Bake for about 1 hour.

▦ INGREDIENTS

2 1/2 cups of sugar
2 cups of cooked pumpkin purée
1 cup of oil
4 eggs
3 1/2 cups of flour
1 teaspoon of baking powder
2 teaspoons of baking soda
1 1/2 teaspoons of salt
1/2 teaspoon of ground cloves
1 teaspoon of nutmeg
1 teaspoon of cinnamon
1 teaspoon of ground allspice
2/3 cup of water
1/2 cup of raisins
1/2 cup of chopped nuts

MAKES 2 LOAVES

BUTTERCUP BREAD

Preheat the oven to 350° F.

(1) Combine the yeast and water in a small bowl and let sit for 5 minutes.
(2) Mix together the flour, sugar, nutmeg, and salt.
(3) In a large bowl, combine the butter and squash.
(4) Add the yeast and flour mixtures to the squash; combine.
(5) If the dough is sticky, add more flour to make the dough soft and smooth.
(6) Knead for 4 minutes and place in a lightly greased bowl.
(7) Cover with plastic wrap, place in a warm draftless corner and let rise until double the bulk.

(8) Punch down and knead for 7 minutes.
(9) Let the dough rise again in the greased bowl cover with plastic wrap until doubled in bulk.
(10) Punch the dough down again and knead for 4 minutes.
(11) Place dough in a lightly greased loaf pan
(12) Cover with plastic wrap and let rise again.
(13) Remove plastic wrap and brush top of loaf with melted butter.
(14) Bake for 40 minutes or until the loaf sounds hollow and is golden brown.

◈ INGREDIENTS

2 1/4 teaspoons of active dry yeast
1/4 cup of water at 80° F.
3 cups of flour
3 tablespoons of sugar
1 teaspoon of nutmeg
1 1/2 teaspoons of salt
2 tablespoons of butter, melted
1 cup of cooked buttercup squash
   purée
1 tablespoon of melted butter

*Life on a pumpkin farm in most cases can
stretch to at least three generations and
sometimes four.*

MAKES 1 LOAF

SAVORY PUMPKIN PUFFS

Preheat the oven to 400° F.

(1) Melt the butter in a heavy enameled Dutch oven.

(2) Add the onion and garlic; cook until the onion is transparent over medium heat.

(3) Combine the mace, nutmeg, cinnamon, brown sugar, horseradish, and ground mustard.

(4) Add to the onion mixture and continue to cook low heat for another minute.

(5) Add the pumpkin purée and cook until heated through.

(6) Transfer to a container, cover, and refrigerate overnight.

(7) Add cheese to pumpkin mixture.

(8) Defrost pastry and roll out until 1/8-inch thick.

(9) Cut with large round cookie cutter.

(10) Place a little less than a tea spoon of pumpkin mixture on each circle of dough.

(11) Moisten edges of pastry and seal each puff into half moons.

(12) Bake for 15 minutes or until golden brown.

(13) Cool for 5 minutes and serve.

INGREDIENTS

2 tablespoons of butter
1 small yellow onion, minced
1 clove of garlic, minced
1/4 teaspoon of mace
1/4 teaspoon of nutmeg
1/4 teaspoon of cinnamon
2 tablespoons of brown sugar
2 teaspoons of horseradish
1/2 teaspoon of ground mustard
1 cup of cooked pumpkin purée
3/4 cup of grated Mozzarella
   cheese
2 packages of frozen Puff Pastry

MAKES 40 PUFFS

PUMPKIN PATÉ

(1) In a saucepan, combine the squash, butter, lemon juice, dill, and 1 1/4 cups of chick stock; cook over medium heat for 5 minutes.
(2) In a separate saucepan, pour in the remaining chicken stock.
(3) Sprinkle the gelatin on top of the chicken stock and let stand for 1 minute.
(4) Heat the gelatin mixture over low heat to dissolve the gelatin.
(5) Add the gelatin mixture to the squash mixture; combine.
(6) Pour the mixture into a mold, cover with plastic wrap and chill until firm.
(7) Garnish with a sprig of dill.
(8) Serve with toasted slices of French bread.

INGREDIENTS

1 cup of cooked butternut squash purée
3 tablespoons of butter
3 tablespoons of lemon juice
3 tablespoons of chopped fresh dill
1 1/2 cups of chicken stock
1 package of unflavored gelatin
1 sprig of dill
1 large loaf of French bread

SERVES 8

PUMPKIN CHUTNEY WITH CREAM CHEESE

(1) In a small saucepan, combine the butternut squash and vinegar; cook until fork tender.
(2) Cut jalapeño pepper in half and carefully remove the seeds; place in the bowl of a food processor.
(3) Cut orange, with rind, in chunks; place in the bowl of a food processor.
(4) Add sugar and water to bowl of the food processor and blend.
(5) Add the pepper and orange mixture to the butternut squash; combine.
(6) Pour this mixture into a bowl and chill for at least 4 hours.
(7) Unwrap the cream cheese and let stand on the counter at least 2 hours before serving.
(8) Pour the squash mixture over the cream cheese and serve with crackers.

INGREDIENTS

1 cup of finely chopped butternut squash
1 tablespoon of white balsamic vinegar
1 jalapeño pepper
1/2 of an orange
1/2 cup of brown sugar
1 tablespoon of water
16 ounces of cream cheese
crackers

SERVES 12

CREAM OF PUMPKIN SOUP

(1) Prepare pumpkin from the Cooking Tips on page 25. You should have about 2 cups of pumpkin purée.
(2) Melt the butter in a heavy Dutch oven.
(3) Add the onions and cook until transparent.
(4) Add the pumpkin, sugar, allspice, and chicken broth and bring to a boil.
(5) Add the cream and reheat but do not boil.
(6) Season to taste with salt and pepper.
(7) Serve garnished with parsley.

 INGREDIENTS

1 small cheese pumpkin
3 tablespoons of unsalted butter
1/2 cup of finely chopped onion
1/2 teaspoon of sugar
1/4 teaspoon of ground allspice
3 cups of chicken broth
1/2 cup of light cream
salt and pepper
parsley, chopped

SERVES 6

CREAM OF PUMPKIN SOUP
WITH RICE

(1) Melt the butter in a heavy Dutch oven.
(2) Add the onions and cook until transparent.
(3) Add the chicken broth, pumpkin purée, nutmeg, lemon zest, cayenne pepper brown sugar, and rice.
(4) Cover and cook over low heat for 25 minutes or until the rice is tender.
(5) Add milk and heat until warmed through.
(6) Serve garnished with cilantro.

INGREDIENTS

3 tablespoons of butter
1 medium onion, chopped fine
3 3/4 cups of chicken broth
2 cups of cooked pumpkin purée
1/4 teaspoon of nutmeg
lemon zest from 3/4 of 1 lemon, grated
1/8 teaspoon of cayenne pepper
2 tablespoons of brown sugar
3 tablespoons of uncooked rice
1 cup of milk
cilantro

SERVES 4

LEEK AND PUMPKIN SOUP

(1) Melt the butter in a heavy Dutch oven.
(2) Add the leeks and saute slowly, over low heat until they are tender but not brown.
(3) Stir in the garlic and continue to cook for 2 minutes.
(4) Add the pumpkin and water; cover and simmer until the pumpkin is tender, about 40 minutes.
(5) Remove from the heat and allow the mixture to cool for 15 minutes.
(6) Purée the mixture in batches in a blender or food processor.
(7) Return purée to the pot, add the cream and season to taste with salt and pepper.
(8) Reheat before serving.
(9) Serve garnished with the minced chives.

INGREDIENTS

2 tablespoons of butter
4 large leeks, white part only, sliced
2 cloves of garlic, minced
3 cups of cubed pumpkin
3 cups of water
1 cup of cream
salt and pepper
1 tablespoon of minced fresh chives

SERVES 4

CURRIED
BUTTERNUT SQUASH SOUP

(1) Melt the butter in a heavy Dutch oven.
(2) Add the onions and garlic and cook until the onion is transparent.
(3) Whisk in the curry to form a paste.
(4) Slowly whisk in the chicken broth.
(5) Add the butternut squash and cook for 10 minutes.
(6) Remove from the heat and allow the mixture to cool for 15 minutes.
(7) Purée the mixture in batches in a blender or food processor.
(8) Return purée to the pot, and heat.
(9) Add the milk and heat until warmed through.
(10) Serve immediately.

INGREDIENTS

3 tablespoons of unsalted butter
1 small onion, chopped fine
1 clove of garlic, minced
2 1/2 teaspoons of curry
4 cups of chicken broth
2 cups of cooked butternut
   squash purée
3/4 cup of milk

SERVES 4

BUTTERNUT SQUASH SOUP
SENEGALESE

(1) Melt the butter in a heavy Dutch oven.

(2) Whisk in the curry and flour.

(3) Cook over low heat for 3 minutes.

(4) Combine 2 cups of the chicken stock and all of the butternut squash and purée in a blender.

(5) Gradually add the purée to the curry mixture, whisking after each addition.

(6) Add the remaining chicken stock and cook over medium heat for 10 minutes.

(7) Add the lemon juice and stir to combine.

(8) Stir in the cream and cook until heated through.

(9) Garnish with parsley and serve immediately.

INGREDIENTS

3 tablespoons of unsalted butter
1 1/2 teaspoons of curry
2 tablespoons of flour
3 3/4 cups of chicken stock
1 cup of cooked butternut squash purée
1 tablespoon of freshly squeezed lemon juice
1/2 cup of heavy cream
parsley

SERVES 6

THE PUMPKIN TUREEN

(1) Cut off top of pumpkin and scoop out the seeds and stingy part.

(2) Rub the interior of the pumpkin with the butter.

(3) Add the onion, horseradish, mustard, evaporated milk, rye bread, salt, pepper, cayenne, nutmeg, and swiss cheese.

(4) Place a piece of tin foil larger than the opening over the top of the pumpkin and then replace the top.

(5) Place the Pumpkin Tureen in a cooking tray.

(6) Bake for 2 hours or until the pumpkin becomes tender. To test remove the lid and pierce the side of the pumpkin with a fork. You should feel scant resistance.

(7) To serve, scoop deeply into the pumpkin scrapping both the sides and bottom to remove the pumpkin meat as well as the soup.

INGREDIENTS

1 pumpkin, 3-4 pounds
1 tablespoon of butter, softened
1/4 cup of very finely minced onion
1 teaspoon of prepared horseradish
1 teaspoon of mustard
13 ounces of lowfat evaporated milk
2 slices of rye bread with caraway seeds, cubed
a dash of salt
a dash of pepper
a dash of cayenne pepper
a dash of nutmeg
1/2 cup of grated swiss cheese, firmly packed

SERVES 4

CREAM OF PUMPKIN SOUP
WITH CINNAMON

(1) Melt the butter in a pot.

(2) Add the onions and cook until transparent.

(3) Add 1 cup of chicken broth and bring to a boil.

(4) Reduce heat and simmer for 15 minutes.

(5) Remove the pot from heat and allow to cool for 15 minutes.

(6) Purée the onion mixture in a blender .

(7) Add the remaining chicken stock.

(8) Combine pumpkin purée, cinnamon, nutmeg, ginger, and pepper.

(9) Add the pumpkin mixture to the onion mixture.

(10) Bring to a boil then reduce heat and simmer for 10 minutes.

(11) Stir in the milk and cream and heat until warmed through.

(12) Cut the bread with a heart shaped cookie cutter.

(13) Place hearts on a cookie sheet and toast one side under the broiler.

(14) Combine the butter, brown sugar, and cinnamon.

(15) Spread butter mixture on the untoasted side of each heart and toast under the broiler until topping is bubbly.

(16) Garnish each serving of soup with a toasted cinnamon heart.

INGREDIENTS

2 tablespoons of butter
1 cup chopped onion
2 1/2 cups of chicken broth
1 cup of cooked pumpkin purée
1/4 teaspoon of ground cinnamon
1/4 teaspoon of ground nutmeg
1/4 teaspoon of ground ginger
1/4 teaspoon of pepper
2 cups of milk
1 cup of heavy cream

4 slices of good quality white
  bread
3 tablespoons of butter, softened
1 tablespoon of brown sugar
1/4 teaspoon of ground cinnamon

SERVES 8

ROASTED BUTTERNUT SQUASH
WITH ROSEMARY

Preheat the oven to 375° F.

(1) Peel the squash with a vegetable peeler.
(2) Cut each peeled squash in half lengthwise and remove the seeds and stringy part.
(3) Cut the bulb end of the squash into four equal pieces. Cut the remaining section of the squash into slices.
(4) Place squash in a baking dish and brush each piece with the melted butter.
(5) Sprinkle rosemary onto squash sections.
(6) Place the baking dish in the center of the oven.
(7) Bake the squash for 35 minutes or until golden.

INGREDIENTS

2 small butternut squash
4 tablespoons of butter, melted
2 teaspoons of chopped fresh rosemary

SERVES 4

STUFFED ACORN SQUASH

Preheat the oven to 350° F.

(1) Place the currants in a small bowl; cover with apple brandy.
(2) In a large saucepan, melt the butter.
(3) Add the thyme, parsley, onion, and celery; cook until the onion is transparent.
(4) Add the bread cubes and stir to combine.
(5) Add the chicken stock and combine.
(6) Cut the acorn squash in half and bake cut side down for 25 minutes.
(7) Remove squash from the oven.
(8) Turn each squash half over and stuff with stuffing.
(9) Cover with aluminum foil and return the squash to the oven; continue cooking for another 15 minutes.
(10) Uncover and cook until golden on top, approximately another 5 minutes.

INGREDIENTS

1/4 cup of dried currants
3 tablespoons of apple brandy
5 tablespoons of butter
1 teaspoon of dried thyme
1 teaspoon of dried parsley
1 cup of diced onion
1/4 cup of diced celery
6 slices of white bread, cubed and toasted
3/4 cup of chicken stock
3 acorn squash

SERVES 6

BUTTERNUT SQUASH
WITH WALNUTS AND RAISINS

Preheat the oven to 350° F.

(1) In a large bowl, combine the squash, butter, and sugar.
(2) Add the nuts and raisins to the squash mixture; mix well.
(3) Pour the squash mixture into an ungreased casserole dish.
(4) Dot with small pieces butter.
(5) Bake for 30 minutes.

INGREDIENTS

5 cups of cooked butternut squash purée
5 tablespoons of butter, melted
1/2 cup of brown sugar
1/2 cup of coarsely chopped walnuts
1 cup of raisins
1 tablespoon of butter

SERVES 8

ROASTED ACORN SQUASH
WITH APRICOTS

Preheat the oven to 375° F.

(1) Slice squash crosswise into 1/4-inch slices.
(2) Place squash in a baking dish and brush each slice with the melted butter.
(3) Bake for 15 minutes.
(4) Meanwhile, heat the jam to a liquid state.
(5) Remove squash from oven, turn each slice over and brush with the remaining butter.
(6) Return to the oven and bake for another 15 minutes.
(7) Remove squash from oven and adjust oven temperature to broil.
(8) Brush each slice of squash with the jam.
(9) Broil until golden.

 INGREDIENTS

2 acorn squash
6 tablespoons of butter, melted
2 tablespoons of apricot jam

SERVES 4

SPICY RICE

(1) Melt the butter in a heavy Dutch oven.
(2) Add the onions and garlic and cook until transparent.
(3) Add the apples and stir to coat with butter.
(4) Add the chicken stock.
(5) Combine pumpkin purée, nutmeg, and cayenne pepper.
(6) Add pumpkin mixture to the onion mixture; stir to combine.
(7) Add milk and cook for 20 minutes.
(8) Meanwhile, combine water and butter in a saucepan, cover and bring to a boil over high heat.
(9) Add rice, reduce the heat and simmer slowly for 20 minutes or until tender.
(10) Add the cooked rice to the pumpkin mixture and stir to combine.
(11) Serve garnished with parsley.

◫ INGREDIENTS

4 tablespoons of butter
1 small onion, sliced and quartered
1 clove of garlic, minced
2 small McIntosh apples, peeled, cored, and chopped
1/2 cup of chicken stock
1/2 cup of pumpkin purée
1/4 teaspoon of nutmeg
1/4 teaspoon of cayenne pepper
1/4 cup of milk
2 cups of water
2 tablespoons of butter
1 cup of uncooked rice
parsley sprigs

SERVES 6

BUTTERNUT SQUASH FRITTERS

(1) Sift together the flour, salt, baking powder, and thyme.
(2) In a large bowl combine the squash, butter, scallions, milk, and eggs.
(3) Add the flour mixture to the squash mixture.
(4) Heat the oil in a cast iron skillet.
(5) When the surface is very hot, pour a small amount of the batter onto the griddle for each fritter and cook until small bubbles appear and begin to break.
(6) Flip the fritters and cook on the other side until golden brown.
(7) Serve immediately.

INGREDIENTS

1 1/2 cups of flour
1/2 teaspoon of salt
1/4 teaspoon of baking powder
1 teaspoon of thyme
1 cup of cooked butternut squash purée
2 tablespoons of butter, melted
3 scallions with 3 inches of green
1 1/2 cups of milk
2 eggs, lightly beaten
oil

SERVES 8

PUMPKIN BREAD PUDDING

Preheat the oven to 350° F.

(1) Toast and tear the bread into bite size pieces.
(2) Melt the butter in a heavy Dutch oven and then add the oil.
(3) Add the onions and garlic cook until the onions are transparent.
(4) Add the thyme, rosemary, and mace and continue to cook for 2 minutes.
(5) Meanwhile, in a large bowl combine the butter, pumpkin purée, chicken stock, eggs, and milk.
(6) Add onion mixture to the pumpkin mixture; stir to combine.
(7) Add bread and stir until well mixed.
(8) Pour the mixture into a deep casserole dish.
(9) Bake in the middle of the oven for 45 minutes or until golden and crispy on top.
(10) Serve immediately.

◈ INGREDIENTS

12 slices of day old bread
2 tablespoons of butter
2 tablespoons of olive oil
3 medium onions, thickly sliced and quartered
2 cloves of garlic, minced
1/2 teaspoon of thyme
1 teaspoon of rosemary
1/4 teaspoon of mace
4 tablespoons of butter, melted
1 cup of cooked pumpkin purée
2 cups of chicken stock
3 eggs, lightly beaten
1/2 cup of milk

SERVES 6

ROASTED WINTER VEGETABLES

(1) Peel and cube the squash, being sure to discard the seeds and stringy part.
(2) Peel and cube the turnip.
(3) Peel and cut the carrots into 1-inch pieces.
(4) Cut the potatoes into cubes.
(5) Peel and cut the onions in quarters.
(6) Cut the celery into 1-inch pieces.
(7) Place all the vegetables in a large enough baking dish to accommodate one layer of vegetables.
(8) Sprinkle the rosemary on top of the vegetables.
(9) Drizzle the olive oil on top and mix to coat all the vegetables with the oil.
(10) Pour the chicken stock over vegetables.
(11) Bake for approximately 45 minutes to 1 hour. Toss the vegetables occasionally to prevent burning.

INGREDIENTS

1 small butternut squash
1 small turnip
6 carrots
4 red potatoes
4 medium yellow onions
4 stalks of celery
1 tablespoon of rosemary
1/2 cup of olive oil
1/2 cup of chicken stock

SERVES 6

BAKED ONIONS

Preheat the oven to 375° F.

(1) Bring a large pot of water to a boil.
(2) Meanwhile, peel off the outer skin of onions.
(3) Cut of a bit of the root end so the onion will sit up.
(4) Cut an X in the root end of each onion.
(5) Gently boil the onions for 12 minutes.
(6) Remove the onions from the water and place in a bowl full of cold water.
(7) When the onions are cool enough to handle remove; scoop out the centers with a melon baller and reserve.
(8) Melt the butter in a skillet and add the reserved onion centers, thyme, and brown sugar.
(9) Saute until the onions are transparent.
(10) Remove the mixture from the heat; cool for 15 minutes and then process in a food processor.
(11) Combine the squash, bread crumbs, cinnamon, nutmeg, and onion mixture.
(12) Stuff each onion with the squash mixture and .
(13) Cover tightly and bake for 40 minutes.
(14) Uncover and top each onion with a small pat of butter; continue baking for another 20 minutes.
(15) Serve immediately with any leftover stuffing.

INGREDIENTS

6 large Vidalia onions
1 tablespoon of butter
1 1/2 teaspoons of thyme
1 tablespoon of brown sugar
1 cup of cooked butternut
    squash purée
1 cup of fine bread crumbs
1 teaspoon of ground cinnamon
a pinch of ground nutmeg
butter

SERVES 6

ROASTED WINTER VEGETABLE LASAGNA

Preheat the oven to 350° F.

(1) Cut top 1/4-inch from the top of the head of garlic just exposing the tops of each clove.

(2) Cut top 1/4-inch from the top of each onion.

(3) Place garlic and onion in a baking dish and brush each vegetable with olive oil.

(4) Add just enough water to coat the bottom and cover the baking dish foil.

(5) Bake for 1 1/4 hours or until the vegetables are soft.

(6) When done squeeze the cloves and onions from their skins and purée in a food processor or blender.

(7) Cook the pasta for 3 minutes and drain.

(8) Combine the garlic mixture, squash, butter, and chicken stock.

(9) Combine eggs, ricotta cheese, rosemary, thyme, parsley Parmesan cheese, and 1 cup of mozzarella cheese.

(10) Coat bottom of a 13x9-inch baking dish with the vegetable sauce.

(11) Cover with 4 lasagna noodles.

(12) Spread half of the ricotta mixture over the lasagna noodles.

(13) Repeat the layers of sauce, noodles, and ricotta.

(14) Top with remaining sauce and sprinkle with the remaining mozzarella.

(15) Cover loosely with foil and place on a baking sheet.

(16) Bake for 40 minutes and remove foil.

(17) Continue baking until golden brown on top

◈ INGREDIENTS

1 head of garlic
2 large yellow onions
8 lasagna noodles
3 cups of cooked butternut
   squash purée
3 tablespoons of butter, melted
2 1/2 cups of chicken stock
2 eggs
3 1/2 cups of ricotta cheese
1 1/2 teaspoons of rosemary
1 teaspoon of thyme
1 tablespoon of parsley
1/4 cup of Parmesan cheese
3 cups of mozzarella cheese

SERVES 8

GARDEN SALAD
WITH PUMPKIN BREAD CROUTONS

(1) Wash and tear the lettuce into bite size pieces.
(2) Slice the onions paper thin.
(3) In the bowl of a food processor add the garlic, rosemary, parsley, basil, sugar, water, and lemon juice.
(4) Add the oil in a slow steady stream.

Preheat the oven to 350° F.

(5) Combine the garlic, butter and cinnamon.
(6) Coat each slice of bread with the mixture using a brush.
(7) Cut each slice of bread into 12 cubes.
(8) Bake for 15 minutes or until the cubes are golden brown.
(9) Arrange the lettuce on salad plates, top with onions and then the croutons.
(10) Drizzle the salad dressing on top and serve.

▨ INGREDIENTS

1 head of red leaf bibb lettuce
1/2 red onion
1 clove of garlic
1 tablespoon of freshly chopped rosemary
2 teaspoons of freshly chopped parsley
1 tablespoon of freshly chopped basil
1 teaspoon of sugar
1/4 cup of water
1 tablespoon of lemon juice
1/3 cup of olive oil
1/2 teaspoon of crushed garlic
8 tablespoons of butter
1 teaspoon of cinnamon
4 slices of Buttercup Bread (see page 32)

SERVES 6

BUTTERCUP MARMALADE

(1) In a medium bowl, mix the squash with the sugar.
(2) Cover with plastic wrap and chill overnight.
(3) Thinly slice and quarter the unpeeled oranges and lemons.
(4) Remove inside core from each piece of orange and lemon.
(5) In a large saucepan, combine the squash mixture with the oranges and lemons.
(6) Bring mixture to a boil.
(7) Boil rapidly for 20 minutes, skimming off scum as necessary.
(8) Pour into hot sterilized jars and top with melted paraffin wax.

INGREDIENTS

4 cups of grated buttercup squash
3 3/4 cups of sugar
2 oranges
1 lemon

MAKES 3 1/2 CUPS

PETER PIPER'S PUMPKIN PICKLES

(1) Wash the pumpkin, peel, and cut into 1-inch cubes.
(2) In a large saucepan or preserving kettle, combine the salt, cinnamon sticks, allspice, cloves, vinegar, and sugar.
(3) Bring this mixture to a boil, stirring constantly, until the sugar has dissolved.
(4) Add the pumpkin chunks to the syrup. and cook for about 10 minutes or until the pumpkin is tender and appears glassy.
(5) Ladle the pumpkin and syrup into hot, sterilized jars to within 1/2-inch of the top.
(6) Wipe the tops and threads of the jars with a camp cloth.
(7) Put the lids and screw tops in place.
(8) Process in a hot water bath for 5 minutes.
(9) Remove jars from the hot water bath and let cool in a draftless spot for 12 hours.

INGREDIENTS

3 pound cheese pumpkin
1 1/2 teaspoons of salt
2 cinnamon sticks
1 1/2 teaspoons of allspice
1/2 teaspoon of whole cloves
2 cups of white vinegar
4 cups of granulated sugar

MAKES 4 PINTS

PUMPKIN COOKIES

Preheat the oven to 400° F.

(1) Mix sugar, shortening, eggs, and pumpkin thoroughly.
(2) Blend together flour, baking powder, cinnamon, nutmeg, salt, and ginger.
(3) Combine pumpkin and flour mixtures.
(4) Add raisins and nuts
(5) Drop the batter by rounded teaspoonfuls onto an ungreased baking sheet.
(6) Bake for 12-15 minutes, or until lightly browned.

INGREDIENTS

1 1/2 cups of brown sugar
1/2 cup of shortening
2 eggs
1 3/4 cups of cooked pumpkin purée
2 3/4 cups of flour
1 teaspoon of baking powder
1 teaspoon of cinnamon
1 teaspoon of nutmeg
1/2 teaspoon of salt
1/4 teaspoon of ginger
1 cup of raisins
1 cup of chopped nuts

MAKES 6 DOZEN

PUMPKIN SHORTBREAD
DELIGHTS

Preheat the oven to 400° F.

(1) In a small bowl, cream the butter.
(2) Gradually add the granulated sugar and vanilla extract.
(3) Continue beating until the mixture is light and fluffy.
(4) Add the flour and mix well.
(5) Press this mixture into the bottom of a 13x9-inch baking dish.
(6) Bake in the middle of the oven for 5 minutes; remove from oven.
(7) Reduce oven temperature to 350° F.
(8) In a small bowl combine the flour, baking powder, and salt.
(9) In a large bowl combine the eggs, brown sugar, pumpkin purée, and vanilla extract.
(10) Add the dry ingredients and nuts to the pumpkin mixture and blend well.
(11) Spread the pumpkin mixture over the crust.
(12) Combine the flour and sugar.
(13) Cut in the butter using two forks or a pastry blender until the mixture resembles a course meal.
(14) Sprinkle this mixture over the pumpkin layer.
(15) Bake for 25-30 minutes.
(16) Remove from the oven and cool on a rack.
(17) When cool cut into squares.

◈ INGREDIENTS

Crust

1/2 cup of butter
1/3 cup of sugar
1/4 teaspoon of vanilla extract
1 cup of flour

Filling

1/2 cup of flour
1/2 teaspoon of baking powder
1/4 teaspoon of salt
2 eggs, slightly beaten
1 cup of brown sugar
1 cup of cooked pumpkin purée
1/2 teaspoon of vanilla extract
1/2 cup of chopped pecans

Topping

1 cup of flour
1/3 cup of granulated sugar
1/4 cup of butter

MAKES 2 DOZEN

OATMEAL PUMPKIN COOKIE

Preheat the oven to 350° F.

(1) Combine flour, oats, baking soda, cinnamon, and salt.

(2) In a small bowl, cream the butter.

(3) Gradually add the brown sugar then the granulated sugar, continue beating until the mixture is light and fluffy.

(4) Add the egg and vanilla; mix well.

(5) Alternately add some of the flour mixture and then the pumpkin. Be sure to blend the mixture well after each addition.

(6) Fold in the chocolate morsels.

(7) Drop the batter by rounded teaspoonfuls onto a lightly greased baking sheet.

(8) Bake for 12-15 minutes, or until lightly browned.

(9) Remove the cookies and cool on racks.

▦ INGREDIENTS

2 cups of flour
1 cup of raw old-fashioned oats
1 teaspoon of baking soda
1 teaspoon of ground cinnamon
1/2 teaspoon of salt
1 cup of butter, softened
1 cup of brown sugar, firmly packed
1 cup of granulated sugar
1 egg, slightly beaten
1 1/2 teaspoons of vanilla extract
1 cup of cooked pumpkin purée
1 cup of semi-sweet chocolate morsels

MAKES 40 COOKIES

PUMPKIN CAKE

Preheat the oven to 350° F.

(1) Sift together the flour, baking powder, baking soda, salt, cloves, allspice, and cinnamon into a large bowl.
(2) Make a well in the dry ingredients.
(3) Add the eggs, sugar, pumpkin, oil, water, nuts, and chocolate morsels; blend until the ingredients are moistened.
(4) Grease and flour a bundt pan.
(5) Pour the dough into the bundt pan.
(6) Bake for 1-1 1/2 hours.
(7) When the cake tests done, cool upsidedown on top of a wine bottle.
(8) Remove the cake from the pan.
(9) Sprinkle with confectioners' sugar

⬕ INGREDIENTS

3 1/2 cups of flour
1/2 teaspoon of baking powder
2 teaspoons of baking soda
1 teaspoon of salt
1/2 teaspoon of ground cloves
1/2 teaspoon of ground allspice
1 teaspoon of cinnamon
4 eggs, lightly beaten
3 cups of sugar
2 cups of cooked pumpkin purée
1 cup of oil
1/2 cup of water
1 cup of chopped walnuts
1/2 cup of chocolate morsels
confectioners' sugar for dusting

SERVES 8

CARAMELIZED CRANBERRY
SUNSHINE CAKE

Preheat the oven to 375° F.

(1) Combine the water, sugar, orange zest, and cinnamon in a pot and heat until the sugar is dissolved.

(2) Add the cranberries and orange sections; cook over moderate heat until cranberries start to pop.

(3) Remove from the heat and strain cranberry mixture reserving 1 cup of the liquid.

(4) In a heavy bottomed skillet, heat sugar over moderate heat until it starts to melt without stirring.

(5) When the sugar starts to melt, stir until all the sugar has dissolved and the mixture is golden brown.

(6) Add the reserved cup of cranberry liquid very slowly to avoid spatters; boil over moderate heat for 6 minutes.

(7) Remove from the heat and pour the liquid into a 13x9-inch baking dish.

(8) Add the cranberry mixture to the baking dish in an even layer.

(9) In a small bowl, cream the butter and sugar together.

(10) Beat the eggs until very light and lemon colored.

(11) Add the eggs to the creamed butter and combine.

(12) In a large bowl, sift together the flour, baking powder, and salt.

(13) Add the squash to the flour mixture; combine thoroughly.

(14) Mix together the hot milk and lemon oil; add to the squash mixture and combine thoroughly.

(15) Pour the cake mixture over the cranberries in an even layer.

(16) Bake for 30 minutes or until a cake tester comes out clean when inserted into the center of the cake.

◈ INGREDIENTS

1 cup of water
2 cups of sugar
grated zest of 1 orange
2 teaspoons of cinnamon
12 ounces of fresh cranberries
1 orange, peeled and sectioned
1 cup of granulated sugar
1/4 cup of butter, softened
1 cup of granulated sugar
2 eggs
1 1/2 cups of pastry flour
2 teaspoons of baking powder
1/2 teaspoon of salt
1/2 cup of cooked butternut
    squash purée
1/2 cup of hot milk
1/2 teaspoon of lemon oil

SERVES 12

PUMPKIN CHEESECAKE

Preheat the oven to 350° F.

(1) In a small bowl mix together the graham cracker crumbs, brown sugar, and cinnamon.

(2) Pour the melted butter over the crumb mixture; mix well.

(3) Press the crumb mixture into the bottom and sides of a 9-inch springform pan.

(4) Bake crust for 7 minutes; remove from the oven and set aside to cool.

(5) Use a mixer to beat together the cream cheese and sugar. Beat for 5 minutes.

(6) In another bowl beat the eggs until fluffy.

(7) While still mixing the cream cheese, add the eggs slowly.

(8) Add the cinnamon, nutmeg, and cloves.

(9) Stir in the pumpkin purée using a wooden spoon.

(10) In a separate bowl, beat the cream until stiff peaks form.

(11) Fold the cream into the cream cheese pumpkin mixture.

(12) Pour the filling into the cooled crust.

(13) Bake for 1 hour.

(14) Remove from oven and cool thoroughly on a rack.

(15) Refrigerate for at least 3 hours or overnight before serving.

 INGREDIENTS

3/4 cup of graham cracker crumbs
2 tablespoons of brown sugar
3 tablespoons of butter
1 teaspoon of cinnamon
20 ounces of cream cheese, softened
1 cup of granulated sugar
3 eggs
1 teaspoon of ground cinnamon
1/2 teaspoon of ground nutmeg
1/4 teaspoon of ground cloves
2 cups of cooked pumpkin purée
3/4 cup of heavy cream

SERVES 10

WHITE CHOCOLATE
PUMPKIN CHEESECAKE

Preheat the oven to 350° F

(1) Combine the pumpkin purée, sugar, ginger, cloves, and cinnamon in a saucepan.

(2) Cook to blend the flavors for about 5 minutes; stirring constantly.

(3) Remove from the heat and cool completely.

(4) Combine the graham crackers and sugar in a small bowl.

(5) Pour the melted butter over the crumb mixture; mix well.

(6) Press the crumb mixture onto the bottom and sides of a 9-inch springform pan.

(7) Bake crust for 10 minutes; remove from the oven and set aside to cool.

(8) Melt the white chocolate in the top of a double boiler over slowly boiling water.

(9) Meanwhile, beat the cream cheese with an electric mixer until smooth and creamy.

(10) Add sugar and mix well.

(11) Add the eggs, one at a time, beating well after each addition.

(12) Gradually add the melted white chocolate.

(13) Pour one-half of the filling into the cooled crust.

(14) Spoon on an even layer of the pumpkin mixture on top of the cream cheese.

(15) Carefully spoon the remaining cream cheese mixture on top of the pumpkin layer.

(16) Bake for 1 hour.

(17) Remove from oven and cool thoroughly on a rack.

(18) Refrigerate for at least 3 hours or overnight before serving.

INGREDIENTS

3/4 cup of cooked pumpkin purée
1/2 cup of granulated sugar
1/4 teaspoon of ground ginger
1/8 teaspoon of ground cloves
1/2 teaspoon of ground cinnamon
1 1/2 cups of graham cracker
  crumbs
4 tablespoons of granulated sugar
5 tablespoons of unsalted butter,
  melted
24 ounces of cream cheese, softened
3/4 cup of granulated sugar
4 eggs
6 ounces of white chocolate

SERVES 10

PUMPKIN-CRANBERRY ROLL

Preheat the oven to 325° F.

(1) Combine the water and sugar; bring to a boil.
(2) Add the orange zest, cinnamon, and cranberries.
(3) Cook until the cranberries loose their shape the sauce thickens.
(4) Set aside to cool.
(5) In a large bowl, mix together the egg yolks, sugar, and pumpkin.
(6) In a small bowl, combine the flour, baking soda, and cinnamon; add to pumpkin mixture.
(7) Beat the egg whites until they form stiff peaks.
(8) Fold the egg whites into the batter.
(9) Pour the batter into a greased jelly roll pan.
(10) Bake for 18 minutes.
(11) Process the cranberry mixture in a food mill.
(12) Combine the cranberry purée, cream cheese, and confectioners' sugar.
(13) Remove cake from the oven and let stand on a cooling rack for 5 minutes.
(14) Place the cake on a towel lightly dusted with confectioners' sugar.
(15) Spread the cream cheese filling evenly over the cake.
(16) Roll the cake using the towel.
(17) Let the cake cool then sprinkle with confectioners' sugar.

☒ INGREDIENTS

4 tablespoons of water
4 tablespoons of sugar
1 teaspoon of orange zest
1/8 teaspoon of cinnamon
1 cup of cranberries
3 eggs, separated
1 cup of granulated sugar
2/3 cup of cooked pumpkin purée
3/4 cup of flour
1 teaspoon of baking soda
1/2 teaspoon of cinnamon
8 ounces of cream cheese, softened
1 cup of confectioners' sugar
confectioners' sugar for dusting

SERVES 8

PUMPKIN CHIFFON PIE

Preheat the oven to 350° F.

(1) Beat the egg yolks until lemon colored.

(2) In the top portion of a double boiler, mix together the egg yolks, brown sugar, pumpkin, milk, salt, and pumpkin pie spice.

(3) Cook over moderate heat until thickened; stirring constantly.

(4) Place cold water in a small saucepan.

(5) Sprinkle the gelatin over the water and let stand for 1 minute.

(6) Cook gelatin mixture over low heat to dissolve granules.

(7) Add gelatin to pumpkin mixture.

(8) Pour the mixture into a large bowl and chill until set.

(9) Combine the graham cracker crumbs and sugar in a small bowl.

(10) Pour the melted butter over the crumb mixture; mix well.

(11) Press the crumb mixture into a pie plate.

(12) Bake the crust for 10 minutes; remove from the oven and set aside to cool.

(13) Combine the egg whites with the remaining 1/4 cup of sugar; beat until stiff peaks form.

(14) Fold egg whites into pumpkin mixture.

(15) Pour the mixture into the graham cracker crust.

(16) Chill until firm.

(17) Serve with whipped cream.

◈ INGREDIENTS

3 eggs, separated
3/4 cup of brown sugar
1 1/2 cups of cooked pumpkin
   purée
1/2 cup of milk
1/2 teaspoon of salt
1 1/2 teaspoons of pumpkin pie
   spice
1/4 cup of cold water
1 package of unflavored gelatin
1 1/2 cups of graham cracker
   crumbs
4 tablespoons of granulated sugar
5 tablespoons of unsalted butter,
   melted
1/4 cup of granulated sugar
whipped cream

SERVES 8

PUMPKIN PIE

Preheat the oven to 450° F.

(1) Blend flour, salt, butter, and shortening with a fork or pastry blender until little "peas" form.

(2) Add water, a little at a time, until dough sticks together.

(3) Roll out dough into a log shape with hands.

(4) Fold log in half and cut at crease.

(5) Form each half of log into a round ball. Reserve one ball, well wrapped, in refrigerator or freezer for another recipe.

(6) With a floured rolling pin on a floured surface, roll the dough out large enough to accommodate the pie plate.

(7) Line a 9-inch pie plate with the pastry; prick the dough all over with a fork, flute the edge with your fingers and chill until ready to add filling.

(8) Combine the pumpkin, sugar, salt, cinnamon, ginger, nutmeg, and cloves in a large bowl.

(9) In another large bowl, beat the eggs with a fork.

(10) Slowly add the evaporated milk to the eggs.

(11) Add the egg mixture to the pumpkin mixture.

(12) Pour the pumpkin filling into the pie shell and place in the oven.

(13) Bake on the bottom rack for 15 minutes, then reduce heat to 300° F. and bake for 45 minutes longer, or until a knife, inserted in the center, comes out clean.

(14) Cool on a wire rack.

(15) Serve slightly warm or at room temperature.

INGREDIENTS

Crust

2 cups of flour
1/2 teaspoon of salt
1/3 cup of butter
1/3 cup of shortening
3 tablespoons of water

Filling

1 3/4 cups of cooked pumpkin
   purée
3/4 cup of brown sugar, firmly
   packed
1/2 teaspoon of salt
1 teaspoon of ground cinnamon
1/2 teaspoon of ground ginger
1/2 teaspoon of ground nutmeg
1/8 teaspoon of ground cloves
2 eggs
1 cup of evaporated milk

SERVES 6-8

PUMPKIN TRIFLE

Preheat the oven to 350° F.

(1) Beat the egg whites until stiff.

(2) While beating, slowly add 5 table-spoons of sugar; set aside.

(3) Combine the lemon juice and egg yolks; beat until lemon colored.

(4) Add lemon rind and sugar; combine.

(5) Carefully fold the egg yolk mixture into the egg whites using a spoon.

(6) Sift the flour 4 times, then sift the flour and salt together.

(7) Fold the flour into the egg mixture.

(8) Pour the batter into two unbuttered 9-inch cake pans.

(9) Bake for 25 to 30 minutes; set aside to cool on a cake rack.

(10) Beat the eggs then pour into the top of a double boiler.

(11) Add the sugar, salt, ginger, cloves, and cinnamon; combine.

(12) Place the top of the double boiler over gently boiling water then gradually add the scalded milk; stirring constantly.

(13) Cook until the mixture has thickened.

(14) Add the pumpkin purée; cook until the mixture coats the back of a spoon.

(15) Add the vanilla extract and combine; set aside to cool.

(16) Heat 1 cup of granulated sugar in a heavy pan over low heat until the sugar is melted and golden. Do not stir sugar until it starts to melt.

(17) Slowly add the boiling water; combine.

(18) Boil for 6 minutes.

(19) Set aside to cool.

(20) Cut one of the cooled sponge cakes into strips and line the bottom of a large glass serving bowl.

(21) Drizzle 2 tablespoons of brandy over the cake.

(22) Spread the 1/2 cup of raspberry jam over the cake.

(23) Pour half of the custard on top of the raspberry jam.

(24) Repeat from step 22 with the remaining ingredients.

(25) Cover the glass bowl with plastic wrap and refrigerate for 4 hours.

(26) When you are ready to serve the trifle, combine the cream and sugar.

(27) Whip the cream until stiff peaks form.

(28) Add the vanilla extract and beat to combine.

(29) Remove the plastic wrap and spoon the whipped cream over the chilled trifle.

(30) Sprinkle cinnamon over the top and serve.

SERVES 8

INGREDIENTS

Sponge Cake
5 eggs, separated
1 cup of granulated sugar
1 tablespoon of lemon juice
lemon zest from 1/2 a lemon, grated
1 cup of pastry flour
1/4 teaspoon of salt

Custard
4 eggs
1/4 cup of granulated sugar
1/8 teaspoon of salt
1/4 teaspoon of ground ginger
1/8 teaspoon of ground cloves
1/2 teaspoon of ground cinnamon
2 1/4 cups of scalded milk
1/2 teaspoon of vanilla extract
1 cup of cooked pumpkin purée

Caramel Sauce
1 cup of granulated sugar
1 cup of boiling water

Whipped Cream
1 cup of whipping cream
1 tablespoon of granulated sugar
3 drops of vanilla extract

4 tablespoons of apple brandy
1 cup of raspberry jam, slightly warmed
cinnamon

PUMPKIN CUSTARD

Preheat the oven to 325° F.

(1) Mix together the pumpkin, bread, egg yolks, Half and Half, sugar, coconut, butter, salt, and orange oil; combine well.
(2) Pour the mixture into a baking dish; bake until slightly browned.
(3) Combine the egg whites and sugar; beat until stiff peaks form.
(4) Remove custard from the oven.
(4) Spread the egg whites on top of the custard.
(5) Return the custard to the oven and bake until slightly browned.
(6) Serve hot or cold.

INGREDIENTS

2 cups of cooked pumpkin purée
1 cup of bread cubes
2 eggs, separated
1 1/2 cups of Half and Half
1 cup of granulated sugar
1/2 cup of shredded coconut
3 tablespoons of butter, melted
1/4 teaspoon of salt
1/2 teaspoon of orange oil
1/4 cup of granulated sugar

SERVES 8

PUMPKIN PIE ICE CREAM

(1) Scald 1 1/2 cups of milk.
(2) In top half of a double boiler, combine the sugar, flour, and pumpkin pie spice.
(3) Add the remaining 1/2 cup of milk to the sugar mixture.
(4) Place the double boiler over medium heat and slowly add the scalded milk.
(5) Add the egg yolks and combine.
(6) Add the pumpkin purée and combine.
(7) Cook until thickened.
(8) Set the mixture aside to cool.
(9) Add the cream, salt, and vanilla extract.
(10) Freeze in a ice cream maker according to the manufacturer's instructions.

◈ INGREDIENTS

2 cups of milk
1 cup of sugar
1 tablespoon of flour
1/2 teaspoon of pumpkin pie spice
3 egg yolks, lightly beaten
1 1/2 cups of cooked pumpkin purée
2 cups of heavy cream
1/8 teaspoon of salt
1 tablespoon of vanilla extract

MAKES 1 1/2 QUARTS

VANILLA ICE CREAM
WITH CARAMEL AND PUMPKIN SWIRL

(1) In a medium saucepan, combine the squash, Half and Half, butter, sugars, and pumpkin pie spice.

(2) Cook over medium heat until all the ingredients are well combined; set aside to cool.

(3) Heat 1 1/2 cups of granulated sugar in a heavy pan over low heat until the sugar is melted and golden. Do not stir sugar.

(4) Slowly add the boiling water; combine.

(5) Boil for 6 minutes.

(6) Slowly add the warmed Half and Half; combine.

(7) Set aside to cool.

(8) In a small bowl, combine the Half and Half, heavy cream, vanilla extract, 3/4 cup of granulated sugar, and salt.

(9) Freeze in a ice cream maker according to the manufacturer's instructions.

(10) Pour one third of the vanilla ice cream into plastic container.

(11) Top with one third of the squash and caramel mixtures.

(12) Pour second third of vanilla ice cream on top.

(13) Top with another third of the squash and caramel mixtures.

(14) Pour remaining vanilla ice cream on top.

(15) Top with the remaining squash and caramel mixtures.

(16) Using a knife, gently swirl the mixtures together.

(17) Place the ice cream container in the freezer.

INGREDIENTS

Pumpkin Swirl

1/2 cup of cooked butternut squash
 purée
2 tablespoons of Half and Half
1 1/2 teaspoons of butter
2 tablespoons of brown sugar
1 tablespoon of granulated sugar
1/8 teaspoon of pumpkin pie spice

Caramel Sauce

1 1/2 cups of granulated sugar
3/4 cup of boiling water
3/4 cup of Half and Half, warmed

Vanilla Ice Cream

3 cups of Half and Half
1 cup of heavy cream
1 tablespoon of vanilla
 extract
3/4 cup of granulated sugar
1/8 teaspoon of salt

MAKES 1 3/4 QUARTS

LEMONY BUTTERNUT SORBET

(1) Combine the sugar and water in a saucepan and bring to a boil.
(2) Boil for 5 minutes.
(3) Add the orange juice, butternut squash, and lemon oil; stir to combine.
(4) Freeze in a ice cream maker according to the manufacturer's instructions.

◈ INGREDIENTS

1 1/4 cups of granulated sugar
2 cups of water
1 cup of orange juice
2 cups of cooked butternut squash purée
1/2 teaspoon of lemon oil

MAKES 1 1/2 QUARTS

PUMPKIN ICE CREAM PIE

Preheat the oven to 350° F.

(1) In a small bowl, combine the graham cracker crumbs and sugar.
(2) Pour the melted butter over the crumb mixture and mix well.
(3) Press the crumb mixture onto the bottom and sides of an 8-inch pie plate.
(4) Bake crust for 10 minutes; set aside to cool thoroughly.
(5) Combine the pumpkin purée, brown sugar, vanilla extract, pumpkin pie spice.
(6) Add the vanilla ice cream; mix well.
(7) Pour ice cream mixture into the cooled pie shell and cover with plastic wrap.
(8) Freeze overnight in the freezer.
(9) Serve with whipped cream.

INGREDIENTS

1 1/2 cups of graham cracker crumbs
4 tablespoons of granulated sugar
5 tablespoons of unsalted butter, melted
1 cup of cooked pumpkin purée
2/3 cup of brown sugar
1/2 teaspoon of vanilla extract
1 1/2 teaspoons of pumpkin pie spice
1 quart of homemade vanilla ice cream, softened
whipped cream

SERVES 8

PUMPKIN BEER

(1) Pour the boiling water into a pot large then add the malt extract , malt, and squash.

(2) Cut a piece of cheesecloth large enough to hold the hops and tie them up into a little bag; add to the above mixture. This is referred to as the mash.

(3) Bring the mash a boil, then reduce heat. Simmer for 1 hour.

(4) Add the ginger root, cinnamon stick, nutmeg, vanilla extract, and finishing hops to the mash.

(5) Simmer the mash for an additional 10 minutes.

(6) Pour off the liquid, referred to as the wort, into the sterilized primary fermentor.

(7) Add enough cold water to make 5 gallons.

(8) Set outside to cool in the winter or place in a sink of cold water.

(9) When the temperature of the wort is below 80° F. add the ale yeast.

(10) Draw off some of the wort into a sterilized hydrometer testing jar, and read its starting gravity. The starting gravity should be between 1.028 and 1.030. If not, slowly add sugar to the wort if it is too low or water if the it is too high until the starting gravity is within the range.

(11) Cover tightly with the lid then apply the air lock.

(12) Place the primary fermentor in a dark place and maintain a temperature of 68° F. to 74° F for 3 to 4 days. When the starting gravity has fallen to 1.020 the wort is ready to be racked.

(14) Three hours before you begin racking, move the primary fermentor onto a counter. This will enable the trub to settle to the bottom.

(15) Racking the beer is done by siphoning off the ale leaving the trub behind. The trub is the thick muddy substance on the bottom of the primary fermentor. To rack the beer, take a shot of vodka and gargle to kill the bacteria in your mouth. Place a carboy racking tube in the primary fermentor. Start the racking by sucking on the other end then place it into the sterilized secondary fermentor.

(16) Add the Irish moss to the wort and cover tightly with the lid then apply the air lock. There should be about 3-inches between the surface of the liquid and the bottom of the lock.

(17) Ferment the beer in a dark place at a constant temperature of 40° to 50° F. until the starting gravity has reached 1.016. This will take at least a week.

(18) Siphon off 2 pints of beer. Warm the beer and then add the priming sugar.

(19) Place the sugar syrup into the sterilized primary fermentor and then rack the beer and stir gently. The starting gravity should increase to 1.021. If it is higher add water.

(20) Sterilize each beer bottle and then thoroughly rinse the bottles to remove all of the sterilizing agent.

(21) Siphon the beer into the bottles using a funnel. Fill the bottles to within 1-inch of the top.

(22) Close each bottle with a crown capping machine.

(23) Store the beer for 1 week at 60° F. to promote fermentation. Then remove beer to a dark spot where the temperature will be between 45° F. to 60° F. The cooler it is the longer the beer will last.

(24) After 10-14 days taste one bottle. Refrigerate for half an hour then carefully pour out the beer leaving behind the sediment. The beer will taste much better after 3 months and even better after 6 months.

Note: Special thanks to Al Krupski for testing this recipe and to Steve Deptula for helping bring this recipe to print.

INGREDIENTS

2 1/2 gallons of boiling water
1 3 1/2 pound can of hopped or uphopped malt extract
1 pound of amber dried malt
1 ounce of hallertaure hops
2 cups of a mixture of cooked butternut and cinderella squash purée
1 ounce of ground ginger root
1 cinnamon stick
3/4 ounce of ground nutmeg
1/2 teaspoon of vanilla extract
1 ounce of fresh dried finishing hops
1 package of ale yeast
1 teaspoon of Irish moss
3/4 cup of priming sugar
Beer making kit

Note: If you are in Brooklyn, New York, try the Pumpkin Beer made by the Park Slope Brewing Co., 356 6th Avenue, Brooklyn, NY 11215 (718-788-1756)

MAKES 5 GALLONS

CHOCOLATE COVERED PUMPKINS

(1) In a large bowl, cream together the butter, squash, and lemon oil.
(2) Slowly add the confectioners' sugar 1 cup at a time; mixing well after each addition. (Towards the end you may want to use your hands.)
(3) Refrigerate for 1 hour.
(4) Roll dough in 1/2-inch balls and refrigerate for another hour.
(5) Bring an inch of water in the bottom of a double boiler to a slow boil.
(6) Melt the chocolate and paraffin in the top of the double boiler over the slowly boiling water.
(7) Dip each ball, one at a time, into the melted chocolate; roll it over using a fork to completely coat.
(8) Remove the chocolate coated ball from the chocolate using a fork.
(9) After the excess chocolate has dripped back into the pan, place the ball on a cookie sheet; repeat from step 7.
(10) Refrigerate until chocolate has hardened.

INGREDIENTS

1 cup of butter, softened
1 cup of cooked butternut squash purée
2 1/2 teaspoons of lemon oil
14 1/4 cups of confectioners' sugar
4 cups of chocolate morsels
4 tablespoons of paraffin

Note: Keep these balls refrigerated until ready to eat.

MAKES 150

ROASTED PUMPKIN SEEDS

Preheat the oven to 375° F.

(1) Remove seeds from the pumpkin.
(2) Rinse the seeds to remove all of the pumpkin strings.
(3) Spread the seeds on a paper towel. Cover with another piece of paper towel and blot the seeds until they are dry.
(4) Spread the seeds on an ungreased cookie sheet.
(5) Bake until the seeds are golden brown; approximately 15 minutes.
(6) Salt to taste.

 INGREDIENTS

seeds from one pumpkin
salt

INDEX

Traditional Country Life Recipe Books from
BRICK TOWER PRESS

Forthcoming titles:

Clambake
Cranberry Companion
Fresh Bread Companion
Soups, Stews, and Chowder Companion

Other titles in this series:

American Chef's Companion
Chocolate Companion
Fresh Herb Companion
Thanksgiving Cookery
Victorian Christmas Cookery
Apple Companion

MAIL ORDER AND GENERAL INFORMATION

Many of our titles are carried by your local book store or gift and museum shop. If they do not already carry our line please ask them to write us for information.

If you are unable to purchase our titles from your local shop, call or write to us.
Our titles are available through mail order. Just send us a check or money order for $9.95 per title with $1.50 postage (shipping is free with 3 or more assorted copies) to the address below or call us Monday through Friday, 9 AM to 5PM, EST. We accept Visa and Mastercard.

Send all mail order, book club, and special sales requests to the address below or call us for a free catalog. We can mail our catalog to you or e-mail a paperfree copy. In any case we would like to hear from you.

You can contact these folks for more information about pumpkins:

Helen Krupski
Krupki's Pumpkin Farm
Main Road, Rt. 25
Peconic, NY 11958
516-734-6847

Vonnie Lawrence
Lawrence Farms
Frozen Ridge Road
Newburgh, NY 12550
914-562-4268

...and for more information about Pumpkin Beer:

Steve Deptula
Park Slope Brewing Company
356 6th Avenue
Brooklyn, NY 11215
718-788-1756

...or anything else:

Brick Tower Press
1230 Park Avenue
New York, NY 10128

Telephone & Facsimile
212-427-7139
800-68-BRICK

E-mail
bricktower@aol.com